Survival

Prepper's Survival Guide - Hunting, Fishing, Canning, and Foraging

Jack Campbell

Jack Campbell

paraphrase any part or the content within this book without the consent of the author or copyright owner. Legal action will be pursued if this is breached.

Table of Contents

Introduction

To begin with, I would like to thank you for choosing and purchasing this book. The uncertainties that life brings have often resulted in several calamities where we have seen loss of life, loss of property and much more. Trouble finds us at the most imperative times leading to inconveniences and so on. We inherently encounter issues everyday in our lives and while some require little thinking and no preparation, some of the bigger ones require lots of preparation. This book ideally talks about the various aspects in which prepping can be useful. It is a handy guide to prepping and survival during times of disasters and calamities.

Prepping is something that is taught in a very basic level at schools and colleges. In fact, certain towns and cities, which are prone to disasters like earthquakes, floods and so on, every family has a survival kit and is ready for action during any disaster that occurs. However, prepping is not an easy overnight task that can be done. It takes a lot of courage and strength both physically as well as emotionally to get over things and have a will to survive. It also takes lots of planning and forethought to be done right.

This book contains four major aspects of prepping. It covers the basics of prepping and survival during times of disasters in the first chapter and proceeds to foraging, hunting, fishing and canning, which are the most important tasks during any calamity or disaster.

It also touches on some tips to remember and gives a brief overview on how to manage during disasters. It takes a holistic approach on prepping and survival skills and throws light on prepping in a way that it is lucid and comprehensive. Please note that reading alone will not suffice and drills and mock practice is required for training. Without much ado, let's move onto the chapters of the book to teach you about surviving those disasters.

Chapter 1
What is Prepping?

So the first question arises, what exactly is prepping and why exactly do we need it? This chapter throws light on just that. It gives a brief overview of what prepping is all about and why it is necessary.

Prepping is preparation. Prepping is to be ready for any disaster that may strike in the future. It is the process of making active preparations for any disaster or an emergency that can strike. The disasters can be both naturally occurring such as earthquakes, floods and so on, as well man-made like terrorism. Prepping gives us three major advantages when a disaster strikes. This is because when any calamity strikes, people rush to the markets and hardware stores hoping to get everything they require like provisions, fixtures, tools, medicine supplies and so on.

The problem is, markets, hardware stores and medicine shops only have a stock of supply and this stock usually sells like hot cakes during disasters and hence one, prices will be extremely high and two, it might get over very soon. During disasters, these places don't have enough supply for meeting the needs of the population.

There are also chances that you might forget what you need due to your fragile state of mind during a disaster and by the time you go back to the stores, chances are the items you require might have already been sold. Thus prepping gives us a basic advantage of having a head start on others. If you already have a lot of supply and all the required medicines, items and provisions that you need, chances are you don't have to worry about getting additional supplies. Also, as soon as disaster strikes, you will have a handy kit of all the items you require, making it easier for you to escape during such events. Thus, your chances of surviving increase when you have everything under control. Also when you prep, you will only have to take care of little things instead of searching for supplies.

Another issue that comes with disasters is that you might have to survive without any technology or electricity and by having a handy survival kit and being well prepared you can meet these unforeseen events. It will also reduce your dependency on emergency services.

Another advantage of prepping is that you will have to experience having no access to modern conveniences that we human inherently depend on. In recent times we have become very dependent on technology and power. We also take them for granted assuming that there will never come a day when we might need to go without them. Thus prepping will help us overcome such dependency and troubles when any disaster strikes.

Now it is not just technology and equipment that is relied on. We also have become dependent on water, food and other basic necessities. We don't realize that some day we might have to do without them and we don't think how we can survive during those times. Prepping solves such problems. Also emergency services can be very problematic. You must have seen during disasters on TV how people had to line up to get provisions like water and food. Rampant fights and arguments break out and people fight for fuel and don't have shelters and several can even die. Think about a time when you will be cut off from civilization and you might not have access to even the most basic of all facilities. That is precisely why prepping for disasters is very important.

Prepping is not hard nor is it expensive. It just requires practice and a clear state of mind. It also requires organizational skills of control and coordination. Prepping is not a new practice though it may seem new and modern to some people. The art of prepping has been developed through several ages. During the World Wars or during any wars in the old days, everyone's pantries would be stocked with canned foods, read to eat supplies, cans of water, fruits and dried vegetables. Candles, dry goods, toiletries, jam and so on would be stocked too.

All the barns would have the equipment and tools to deal with the disasters and barns will even have special cells and rooms for protections against storms or bombings. These bomb shelters were a common feature during both the world wars. Back in the days, people couldn't afford to depend on the government for providing security, safety and provisions. Preppers believe that the responsibility of their safety and security is theirs to bear and believed in self-reliance. They were survivors and did not depend on external factors for protection.

Prepping is a two way process. The first step is mental preparation. Courage and confidence is very important. You need to believe that you can survive and not lose hope. It is important that in order to be safe along with your family members you get rid of unnecessary attachments with materials. You will have to leave behind several expensive or sentimental things but these should be the least of all your worries. The second type of preparation is the physical preparation that you need to do. Ensure that you are well exercised and remember to take adequate nutrients and vitamins at every chance you get. You also need to be flexible and move fast. You can join a track team or go for an athletic class to develop speed and flexibility. Apart from just body strength you will also require to sort out things and you will need energy for this. Throw out unnecessary items and clean out regularly to avoid accumulation.

Jack Campbell

Chapter 2
Foraging For Plants

Most of us are dependent on our surroundings and shops for providing us with foods, groceries and so on. Today, we are exposed to several dangers that can tarnish us and several diseases that can harm us. With the environment becoming exceedingly unpredictable, it is best to be prepared for any impending dangers that may await us. During disasters we are not able to find foods that we can eat and often we end up not having enough food or the food supply runs out. In these cases, knowing how to forage becomes a very useful skill.

Foraging can be defined as that method through which we search for food that is edible. It is primarily associated with forests and camping where we aren't exposed to savvy gadgets and stock of supplies. Foraging is associated with people back in the early days who used to search for food and would go to another area once the food source in a particular area was over. Foraging is not just limited to searching for plants to eat, but it also includes hunting and fishing. In this chapter we are going to be looking at plant foraging primarily and the hunting and fishing will come in the subsequent chapters.

When it comes to foraging, always remember that you are eating for survival. It is a good idea to carry packed foods, canned foods and so on. Carry what you can. The main condition when it comes to foraging is to know if the plant is or is not poisonous. The rule of thumb here is to know all about the plants in your area. When you are trying to survive during disastrous times, the first and foremost step is to not go very far from known areas. Don't try to go into uncharted territories. This is because the plants species you will find here will usually be very different from the plant species in known localities. Determine a good locality to go to and stay there. Take a course or have a handy guide on knowing how to identify plants that can be potentially harmful. Learn about the species in your vicinity. If you know the plants in your locality in and out, you will know what is edible and what is not. Thus you can also be able to avoid the plants that you don't know. When identifying plants also look for their other uses.

Always remember to be well acquainted with the herbs, bushes and trees. Learn and read as much as possible. Take classes on gardening or go for courses on foraging. Try to read all about the plants, forget just identifying those plants, learn about the nutrition associated with the plants, if the plants have any medicinal properties and so on. This will help you because if you ever manage to get hurt in your attempt to survive the disasters then by knowing if the plant is medicinal you can probably apply it or consume it for its medicinal properties.

It is imperative to avoid plants that you cannot identify. Several plants look very similar and if you are not a hundred per cent sure about the plant then it is best to avoid the plant. If it ends up being a poisonous plant then you are doomed. So it is best to stick to known plants. Remember to cross check and recheck the plant to be very sure about its type and if it is edible. Also remember to learn the soil conditions and what plants grow in what soil conditions.

Another rule of thumb to remember to is to know the scientific names of the plants. Common names usually refer to several different types of plants. Some poisonous plants and edible plants can have the same common name but will vary in their scientific names. Usually when looking for plants, if you cannot deal with their scientific names, it is best to choose their Latin names. Latin names of plants do not change and you won't make any mistakes. It is a good idea to get an expert to teach you first hand. This is important when it comes to prepping. You will avoid making mistakes. Another thing is to use all your senses when trying to identify plants. Don't try to just have a visual idea of the plants. Plants may look very similar but their smell, texture and taste may vary. Usually, poisonous plants smell bad and they are rough to touch. Below is gist on how to identify plants

1.   Look at the plant closely. Look at the flowers, the leaves, the roots and so on. This will give you an idea on what type the plant is. If you cannot identify the plant vaguely at this point, it is best to avoid the plant.

2.   Then sniff the plant. Try not to get too close but get a whiff of the plant. Check if you can identify the plant from then on.

3.   Then rely on touch, feel and texture of the plant. Check if the leaves are soft or hard and similarly with flowers and so on.

4.   Finally if you are absolutely sure it is not poisonous take a small bit of the plant. Always remember to rinse and wash the plants several times before using. You don't know what kind of pollution it will have and what dirt it may have. It is a good tip to eat or use one leaf or petal at a time and see if you are developing any sort of allergic reactions to it. The rule of thumb here is to first rub the plant leaf or the petal on your skin and wait for a while to check for any reaction. If you do not face any reaction then rub the petal or leaf on your lips and wait for a while and if you still don't have any reaction try eating a small portion of it and wait to check if you are developing any symptoms.

Now another important thing is to know the habitat of the plant. Apart from just knowing what kind of plants grow in your vicinity, it is a good idea to know the natural habitat of the plant. If you ever happen to get dislocated and have no idea which area you are in, knowing the natural habitat of the plants would help. If you end up in a marshy area, then you should have adequate knowledge to know how to identify marshy plants, similarly with desert plants like cacti and so on. Also get acquainted with plants that grow with a certain type of plants. Usually some plants grow next to each other or they grow in the same vicinity. For instance, when you spot yellow docks you are also likely to spot poke weed in the same vicinity. Also do not underestimate the power of seasons. There are plants that do not grow in every season. Hence, it is important to know what plants grow in what seasons. You don't know when disaster may occur, therefore knowing the plants in all seasons is very important.

Plants change appearance according to seasons so know how to identify the plants in any season. For this purpose it is a good idea to follow the plants throughout all seasons. If you can afford to light a fire then it is always a good idea to boil the plant, its leaves, roots, stems or flowers. This will get rid of any toxic element and get rid of any bacteria that may be clinging onto it. In plants, there are specific parts you can eat and those that you can't. Know the difference as it can literally save your life. You can eat the berries of some plants but you may not be able to eat the leaves of those plants like elderberries. Similarly, some parts of plants can be eaten during certain seasons. Try to get information regarding this also.

Do not forage in toxic areas. This does not just limit to the area but also the place where the plant is growing. If the edibles are growing near the road then chances are the leaves or fruits or whatever the edible parts are may be highly contaminated with lead and you may get lead poisoning. Similarly soil too matters. Avoid pesticide infested areas and areas that are near factories or industries. Water source is important as well. When you go foraging know what the water source is for that particular plant. This is especially important for those plants that are eaten raw. Contaminated water can lead to a lot of problems as well. It is best to stick to plants that look healthy. Do not go for plants that appear sick, decaying or frail. These plants may be infected with some virus or bacteria and may not be good to eat. Doing this will help you reduce the risk of acquiring any illness. Consuming plants that are diseased can also cause death.

Jack Campbell

Chapter 3
Foraging For Water

It goes without saying that water is one of the most important things that we require. A person should drink about a gallon of water each day. The human body is made about more than 75 percent water and hence it is no surprise that water is one of the most important things to look for when surviving. The main thing to remember about water is that one person can go three days without water. Most people die of dehydration due to lack of water. When you do manage to obtain water also caution must be exercised because water can contain several impurities that can cause many diseases and the pathogens and metals found in water can even kill you. In this chapter we look at some basic ways through which you should forage for water.

In the wilderness, your chances of survival depend upon obtaining water. Water can be found in streams and springs. These are the freshest sources of water and it is best to use this water. Another way through which you can obtain water is to collect morning dew. Never collect water from rivers or streams that are situated near industries and factories, but if you must collect that water because it is the only source, and then remember to filter the water. There are several ways through which you can filter water. Filtering pumps and even small chemicals like iodine can help filter the water. During survival situations when disasters strike it is a good idea to carry these. Additionally it is a good idea to carry grapefruit seed. These are said to be able to purify water to a considerable extent though there are debates on how effective it is. If you cannot find ways to purify water and you do not want to waste iodine, then it is a good idea to boil the water before using it. Boiling water for a while will kill out all the viruses and bacteria present in the water.

Make your own water distillery in ten minutes by using two soda bottles. Drill a hole in the caps of both the soda bottles and insert a small tube through each of the caps and down into each of the bottles after placing the caps onto the bottles. Ensure the tubes are about a good few feet. Fill one of the bottles with water you want to filter or distill, bring that tubing that you did and place it in the sunlight and place the tubing of the other bottle in the shade. The sun will heat up the water in the soda bottle, and when the water starts to boil it ends going into a gaseous form when this happens, it expands and rises and goes through the tubes and onto the water bottle placed in the shade. Because the water bottle is in the shade, the water vapor will cool down and settle as drinkable water in the bottle that is placed in the shade. With this method you can also purify salty water, simply put a black cellophane tape around the water bottle placed in the sunlight, this will catch all the salt from the water.

It is always a good idea to carry water and spare water bottles. Remember to store water in your storage house as well. Save up on water for at least 3 gallons of water per person per day.

Jack Campbell

Chapter 4
Basics of Hunting

When you are left in the wilderness or when you have to fend for yourself it is a good idea to know how to hunt. Disasters can occur unexpectedly and if you don't know how to safeguard yourself you might end up being severely injured. In this chapter we will discuss about the basics of hunting.

If you have no prior hunting experiences then make it a point to go for a hunting course or get a mentor who will teach you some basics. It is also known as the hunter's safety course and this is very important, as it will tell you the basics of hunting and the ways in which you can stay safe and not get attacked. There are several courses online but it is important to go for the actual course, which will prep you during times of disasters. When you get a mentor you will be able to be an apprentice and you can learn a lot from the mentor.

You can carry a small gun but it is also a good idea to carry cross bows and other sort of weapons. Practice shooting a couple of times and know what sorts of animals are around. Choose a good area to hunt. It is a good idea to know the behavior patterns of animals. So study these patterns to know which one will suit you the best. Usually look for edible plants; these patches are where the animals are usually around. Remember that the forests change from season to season and so when you are in the wilderness, look for areas where there is a lot of foliage, berries and adequate sunlight. These spots usually have animals that come to graze. Now another important thing to note is the animals may not shelter in the same area all the time. For this purpose, it is important to keep track of the animals throughout the seasons. Look at their feeding patterns, what they eat and how they can in turn be eaten.

When you are practicing, make it a point to identify key areas where animals take shelter and cover. Make a note of these spots. Take a hike through the wilderness and find out the various spots. It is also a good idea to have an aerial map of the wilderness that you might have to escape into. When you have a map, look at possible sources of water and food. The key here is, do not hunt for the animal before you obtain water. Animals usually live in close proximity to water and edible food. So if you can follow it and understand the schedule of it, you will be able to find water and edible plants. This is also very useful if you cannot identify the plants because what plants the animals can eat you can eat as well. Scavenge for news relating to the wilderness or find areas where the trees have fallen or there are several bushes around. Animals usually love to stay in those areas especially deer. This is because they love to stay hidden and watch out for any danger. These areas are also well sheltered and you can utilize these areas for your personal shelter too. Usually the area with thick foliage is where the deer and other small animals prefer living and you can see them in the fall months. During this time period, the weeds and grasses are tall enough to hide the deer and this works in your advantage as a hunter as well. Through the tall blades you can see the animals and hunt them. Pines and young maturing trees also serve as animal shelters and you can look at these spots to know which animals come there.

Keep an eye out for all the natural edible plants and these spots are where animals come to eat. It is a good idea to carry a pair of binoculars in your survival kit as these binoculars can help you spot the animals. Look at the area around and check where you can set your snare or trap. Now there are many different types of hunting. Now realize that shooting is not always an option and you want to minimize shooting the animals when you hunt for food. This is because you want to save the bullets for times of danger to protect yourself and if you do, you might end up giving away your location. In such times, hunting is much more than just mere shooting. Some of the various ways through which you can obtain food from the forest include using a cross bow, snares, traps and so on.

Crossbows are ideally the best type of weapons you can use when you are going hunting. This is because cross bows cause a lot less damage and cause blood loss to the animal. Crossbows are also easier to use than a regular bow and arrow. Remember that knowing where to hit the animal is very important as well. Go to your local archery and find out how to use a crossbow. You can also ask them for recommendations on what cross bow to buy and they will give you plenty of advice and you can even practice with them.

You can also trap animals and these serve as invaluable skills as there are several kinds of traps. Foothold traps are the most common type of traps that are used. These have two jaws attached with a couple of springs, which is triggered in the center. When the trap is stepped on it latches into the animal's foot. The important thing to note about such traps is the size of them. You can get them in your hardware or hunting store. These traps come in different sizes depending on the type of animals that you want to catch; hence it is always a good idea to know what types of animals are around. Also it is important to know the type of animal that you are catching; there are many instances where the animals chew their own foot off to escape. So know what you are dealing with.

There are larger types of catches called cage traps but these traps are usually impractical and cannot be used during a survival streak. However, it is imperative to know about them because you can use them to catch animals like, rabbits, deer, moose, and so on. Dirt hole trapping is another type of trap wherein shovels come very handy. In this you dig a small hole to lure in the animal. Snares are another type of traps where in you have cables or wires that are set up to catch animals like rabbits. These are easy to make and easier to use. You can make your own snare using a couple of wires. It is best to avoid death fall traps as one can get injured when setting this up. It is also quite complicated.

Tips on becoming a better hunter:

•   Human odor can cause alarm in any animal, hence it is best to let yourself soak in the surroundings, and this will reduce the human scent that comes naturally.

•   Remember to carry wires and small knives with you if you are going hunting.

•   Remember to be slow and wear clothes that camouflage you. This will reduce your chances at being spotted by the animals. This will also help you blend into the wilderness during times of danger.

•   When you hear any noise, stop and listen. Animals have an excellent sense of hearing and while a snapped twig is something you might disregard, they wouldn't and they would assume that danger is lurking and hence would go into hiding.

• Always remember to skin the animals and as soon as you catch the animals. Use knives, small glass shards and other tools to skin the animals. Skins usually come off when the animal is warm. This will also get rid of the fleas and any bacteria that are lying on the surface.

Jack Campbell

Chapter 5
Basics of Fishing

When you are trying to survive, you need to ensure that you consume adequate food. It might not be large quantities but it is imperative to take nutritious and healthy food as surviving can take a toll on your physical health and stamina. Fishing is one of the ways through which you can obtain food. Inclement weather also results in health hazards, during times of storms and cyclones; the body starts to use up more nutrients and vitamins to be able to perform simple tasks and to focus. All these require huge amounts of energy. You can obtain this from the food that you gather through hunting, fishing and foraging for edible plants.

If you have to survive in the wilderness then your options are not limited. You can hunt for wild game, forage for edibles plants or fish. The best part is you can load up on nutrients by eating these, as all these sources are fresh food sources. They are high in nutrition and essential vitamins and minerals, thus enabling you to perform better. Fishing does not require adverse technology, which makes it a better option when foraging for food. In this chapter we are going to look at the basics of fishing.

It is important to choose a good spot. Lakes, rivers and streams are the best bet. Ponds can be helpful as well. You can get maximum output from these areas. It is a good idea to go through the various types of fish that are available in the area. This rule applies for foraging when it comes to plants but it is also applicable for other sources of foods like fish and meat. It is a good idea to know your fish, learn about the types of fish and so on. Also when choosing a spot, the ideal spots are usually located where the deep water meets the shallow waters. This is because most fish that you can eat live in the deep waters but will swim towards shallow waters to eat. Usually, look for places where there are foliage, branches and wooden logs. Bugs are usually found in these spots and this where most fish come to feed often.

Once you choose the fishing spot, find the ideal time through which you can fish. Fish usually make an appearance during sunrise and sunset because these periods are not too hot and thus they are the best fishing hours. Fish usually appear at the surface during dawn or dusk. So be alert during these times. If you are eating the fish also look for clean water. Remember to check these beforehand. In your survivor's kit carry a fishing rod. If you are unable to do this, carry fishing lines with you. These fishing lines can be very handy as you can tie them to a large tree branch or a strong twig and use that for fishing with one end having the bait that is tied up.

Alternately instead of a hook you can use a paper clip or a broken top of the can, which is used to pop open the can, a very sharp twig or even bobby pins. If you happen to not carry strings with you, carry at least shoelaces. These can be tied to any of the things that can double up as a fishing hook. Alternatively you can use tall grass or seaweed but these could be tricky to use as they may break under the weight of the fish. Try to use meat as bait. It is a good idea to choose a spot, throw in some scraps of food and wait to check if fish appear in that spot to nibble on the scraps. You can also use colorful bits of plastics as bait. Leaves, dead insects, smaller fish and rotten meat can serve as baits.

If you do not happen to use any of these, you can use the scoop method to gather fish. Simply look for shallow waters for the fish to come. Once you see the fish, take a mug or bucket and scoop it. Tide pools are usually where small clusters of fish live in. You can use the scooping method here effectively. If you find a small low laying area with not much water then you can use this spot to catch fish. Simply try to remove the water using a bucket or a vessel, once the water levels go down you can obtain the fish easily by scooping method.

Remember that the weather can have an effect on the fish as well. Fishing can be affected by the types of changes that occur in the water. When the weather is cold, the fish usually feed earlier in the day and they come near the shore during the daytime when the water is warm.

Learn the behavioral pattern of the fish in the area. When the weather is going to be cold, fish would usually start to eat more at this point. Therefore you can get maximum fish at this time period. When the weather is warm, fish make their appearance and thus it is also a good time to fish. Fish become more active when there are warm spells during cold seasons. When the weather is cloudy, it is a good idea to go fishing. Due to lack of light, fish find it better to come to shore during these periods. When it drizzles, fish cannot see you and you will get concealed. Rain also washes bugs and other baits and this is the time when fish come to feed and you can catch them without them becoming wary of your presence. When there is a storm, fish usually do not appear at the surface during this time. The water also becomes muddy and you will not be able to see anything due to cloudy vision. The bait won't be visible and fish would not come to eat. They also will not remain in place. When the storms arrive along with lightening, do not fish. Get away from the water and go to safe shelters.

Most fish face the current or the wind. This is the case with about 99 per cent of the fish found anywhere. The key here is to place the bait in front of the fish. First try to find the direction of the wind, if you have a fishing rod or a make shift fishing rod you can cast with the wind. The windy conditions also play a pivotal role in pushing the food for the fish including bugs and worm into the water. Hence the fish go in the direction of the wind.

When you fish, it is a good idea to also opt for windy climates. Wind kicks up the waves and the sunlight is largely reduced. This creates a perfect time for fish to swim to shallow waters. They also cannot see or hear your movements. During clear weather, the water is usually stagnant with little to no waves. Fish can easily spot your movement at these times. Also when the water is clear and there is wind, wind usually kicks up all the mud and sediments making the water cloudy and at this time fish don't detect your movement or feel your presence hence you can fish during this time as well.

Chapter 6
Basics of Canning

Canning is an important skill that is required to store your food. Though canning is typically done in factories, you too can learn how to can to store all your food when disaster strikes. In this chapter we are going to look at the basics of canning. Canning has been done for over centuries and it is process of storing food in cans. Back in the days when wars took place, people used to can their food to shield themselves. This is also how farmers used to store their harvest for the winter. Canning is also preserving the food. Now proper canning is quite expensive because of the equipment used. But in order to preserve food using the right equipment and tools is very important. The advantage with canning is that food gets loaded up for months together. There is little chance of wastage and spoilage. Cans of food are shelf stable and portable.

Important thing to note here is that canning should be done properly; when canning is done improperly it can host a variety of bacteria that can do you more harm than good. Hence it is necessary to practice the art of canning. Pressure canning is the most widely used method for canning. Hot water canning is another popular method however this is usually done for jams or other types of acidic food, as they are not a very reliable source of canning. For pressure canning, first take jars and remember to wash them thoroughly, it is important to wash and dry the cans well. Fill them with cooked or raw food. Adding food will help preserve the cans for a longer time so it is a good idea to add a little salt. The salt will also serve as a taste maker for you.

Once you have filled the can, add some vegetable stock or any form of cooking liquid onto the can. You can even add water if you prefer and then just shut the can. Once this is done, secure the can very tightly. Ensure the canner has a good bottom, as the can should not crack in the heat. Start to heat the cans. Most canners have a specific temperature and going above that can increase the pressure inside the can causing it to burst. After this process is done, remove the lid from the heater of the can and let it cool. Once the cans are cool you should hear a sound that signifies a vacuum has been created. This vacuum will press the lid onto the can and secure it more tightly. Now you can store the cans wherever you want.

Meats can be canned through this method. However, if you want to preserve fruits and vegetables it is a good idea to avoid this method of canning as this method can lead your fruits to become soggy and spoilt. It is a good idea instead to store them through alternate ways like jams and preservatives. You can even store them in the form of jellies. Another important thing to note about canning is the storage of the cans. It is a good idea to store cans in the shade where there are no extreme temperatures. Do not keep them in the sun. Usually basements serve as the best places to store them however caution must be exercised as during winter season, basements can become very chilly and the cans run the risk of freezing.

Another method of canning is the hot water canning. In this form of canning, acidic food like pickles, tomatoes, fruits are stored. This is done using acidic ingredients like vinegar, lemon juice or even pectin. This form of canning comes in very handy during survivals. Note that the best and easiest way to can is through the high-pressure canner. In the water bath method of canning, take a large pot with hot water. The pot must be large enough to cover the cans that you intend to put inside. Fill the jars with the various foods that you want to preserve. Screw on the lids and attach the rings onto the cans. Now it is a good idea to keep some sort of rack or have a mechanism to reduce your cans from sinking into the bottom and burning. Heat the pot and let the water start to boil. Put the jars onto the rack or plate at the bottom of the pan and pour some more water about an inch or so to cover the lid of the can. The can should be fully immersed in water. The water must boil and leave it for a while. Once this process is done, take the cans out carefully by using a pair of tongs and let them cool down. Once they complexly cool down you will hear a pop signifying that the lids have been in place and a vacuum has been created.

Rule of thumb here is, if you are storing fruit then they will take any time from 15 minutes to half an hour. Any other products take a much longer time, more than half an hour.

Tips and points to be noted:

•   Make sure that the jars do not have any sort of cracks or marks. Wash everything before using including the rubber ring. Also remember to dry the rubber ring, this is because it can get very moist and several bacteria can leech itself onto the rubber ring making it very unhealthy. Use hot water to clean the cans and dry out in the sunlight.

•   Sterilize all the lids. These are where maximum contaminants are.

•   When you do fill the cans remember to fill all the way but leave an inch on top. Wipe the brims of the cans as well. This will reduce the pressure inside the can while heating.

•   Remove any air bubbles that occur, you can do this by poking the contents of the jar with a chopstick or a stirrer.

•   When you can and if you are not an expert it is a good idea to use recipes that are specially designed for the canning process. This is because while using the water bath method of canning, you would require the right amount of acid to preserve the food. This process of preserving will not occur if you don't know the process properly hence it is a good idea to can using recipes that are custom made for the preserving process.

- Remember to also store market bought cans of foods and ready to eat foods in your shelf. This is also very useful. Do not just simply rely on what you have made. There are chances where your cans might get spoilt or worst, they can get broken. So opt to buy regular cans of preserved food along with your concoctions.

Chapter 7

Managing Disasters

There are times when disasters strike and you will need a lot more skills to manage disasters. This chapter gives a brief overview on what to do when a particular disaster strikes.

Earthquakes

Earthquakes are some of the most common types of disasters that are bound to occur. You can recognize an earthquake by the shaking of the ground. When earthquakes occur it is a good idea to look for an open space and go stand or relocate to that spot. Get away from trees, electric poles, buildings and so on. These may fall and you might die or get severely injured. You can also get under a sturdy desk or crawl under a good bed. This will reduce the chances of things falling on top of you. If you do not find any structures like this, it is a good idea to sit against a wall with your knees up and your head locked between your knees. This will get rid of any falling debris. The debris will not hit your head, which can affect your brain. If you live in an earthquake prone zone then it best to protect yourself by constructing your house with light weight material. This will prevent injuries during earthquakes. Avoid using glass as decorations if you happen to live in such areas. Use fasteners and tapes to secure paintings and other sort of wall hangings, this will minimize loss of items and also they will not fall on you.

Heat Waves

When the temperature of the area you live in starts to soar you know a heat wave is coming your way. Heat waves are usually found in arid dry lands, especially in deserts and in these cases they can result in loss of life due to heat stroke, loss of water causing a drought and loss of flora and fauna. When you find yourself amidst a heat wave get shelter. Go into a house with high roofs. If you live in areas where there is a higher frequency of heat waves then you should build the house with tough material and when a heat wave comes you should seal the house entirely. This is because heat waves usually are accompanied by sand storms and these storms can harm your house and destroy your living space if it gets in. Hence remember to seal the house entirely. Ensure that there is adequate water supply in the house. Store up on water, as this is very important. Droughts can come due to heat waves and you should have a provision where there is water stored in the basement, as these often are the coolest part of the house. Store preserved food and turn on all cooling equipment to cool yourself during these times.

Volcano

Volcanic eruptions are not very easily recognizable though there are three types of volcanoes. It is a good idea to know which category of volcano the mountain or hill located in your region is. If it does happen to be an active volcano then you can recognize an oncoming volcanic eruption through the behavior of animals as they usually flee and are more sensitive to such things. When a volcano erupts it is a good idea to stay indoors. Buildings usually don't run the risk of burning down and so it is best to stay indoors. When a volcano erupts remember to shut and seal all openings including windows or else wear protective goggles and a mask to prevent inhaling toxic fumes. This can cause burns and you might even die from these burns. They also happen to be highly cancerous so always remember to wear your safety gear. Ensure you have sufficient water in your house and store these waters away from walls in the basement. People often think that the volcanic ash can't reach them if they are situated at a high-rise building. However volcanic ash can reach great heights and hence always remember to remain indoor.

Cyclones

Cyclones usually occur when there is low pressure around the water bodies. They may seem like a problem for the oceans but they can result is heavy winds and torrential rainfalls that can severely affect you. If you live near the coast or a have a house that overlooks a water body you can check the movement of the waves and recognize the cyclone. If animals manage to get away you know a cyclone is approaching. In these scenarios, you can expect a power cut and a shortage of supply of basic amenities. Stock up on food and water if you happen to be living in areas where the onset of cyclones is more. Try to store non-perishable ready to eat food. Stock up on candles and have working flashlights. Carry a cigarette lighter with you, as they will help you to navigate during times of power cut. Get away from the house if you have to and reach a high lying area that may be near your residence. If the water body starts to flood you won't have to deal with it. Stock up on all the medicines especially flu tablets as flu usually breaks out during cyclones. It is also a good idea to carry satellite phones as these do not rely on the mobile towers of the regular phones and you can communicate better. Always take your survival kit along with you.

Land Slides

A landslide can occur at any point. This is a common phenomenon that occurs in hilly and mountainous regions of the world. Though they are sudden, they usually occur due to rainfall and avalanches. When this happens it is a good idea to either be indoors or flee from the area. Avoid traveling when there are heavy rains and at the first sight of a drizzle, get shelter. If you must travel during chilly weathers, carry adequate amounts of acid and salt as these help to melt the snow. It is also a good idea to take the same steps as in an earthquake. Get into an open space. If you cannot get into an open space get under a sturdy table or a strong bed to avoid debris falling on top of you. Have enough provisions like water and food to get you through.

Wars and Riots

A conflict that takes place between two large groups of the population is thought of as war and it involves not just physical force but also of weapons and violence. Armed conflict is also one way of defining war and this is done to avoid any unnecessary interference of national or even international law related to warfare. A war that takes place between two or more states and is decided by an official decree and is led by the orders of the governments and the national armies of the countries is referred to as an interstate war. A war that takes place between two parties on opposite sides of an issue within the border of one country is referred to as civil war. At times it may so happen that a civil war in one country might turn into representative wars, in such a case both the opposing parties tend to receive support from external parties that might be representing a particular interest. To understand this better, let us take a look at Korea and Vietnam during the Cold War period. When a conflict involves a small number of sovereign, partisan fighters who are against the ruling government in their country is referred to as Guerilla war. When the population or the people of a country are defending their own state from the occupying state, then such a war is referred to as an independence war or a decolonization war. There can be various reasons for a conflict; some reasons could even be due to economic measures like boycotts or sanctions that are taken by one country against the other. For instance Iraq and Cuba have been affected by the medication boycott by USA; this also results in damage to the population of the country.

When a protest or even an act of civil disobedience spirals out of control takes a violent turn; on purpose, by premeditation or even accidentally, then such an event is referred to as a riot. This violence could be directed towards a hostile group of individuals or even turn towards damaging the immediate physical environment. Riots in general tend to be a mixture of both the scenarios. Riots often take place between two opposing groups such as the left wing activists and neo-Nazis or a riot can occur between protestors who are civilians and the police, paramilitary forces or even the state. For instance the riot that took place between the critics of globalization during the WTO conference that was held in Seattle. The violence during a protest can be started by either of the sides; it could be the protesters or the police force. Motive behind these riots is usually political but it can also be caused due to mass panic like the ones caused during a football match.

Tsunamis

Tsunamis are the enormous waves that are caused because of disturbances under the surface of water such as earthquakes, volcanic eruption or even a landslide. These are also referred to as seismic sea waves. A tsunami is capable of travelling at a speed of more than hundred miles per hour and the waves can be over a 100 feet high. All tsunamis are dangerous but they might not strike all the coastlines in a similar manner. Tsunamis are often generated due to major earthquakes. If a major earthquake or a landslide occurs close to the shore, the first wave might hit the coast way before a warning is issued. You can take a few steps that can help you in protecting yourself, your family and even property from the unpleasant effects of a tsunami. You should prepare a survival kit and make plans with your family for alternative routes of evacuation and communication in case of a tsunami. You should know the height of the area you are residing in above the sea level and its distance from the coast. If you are a tourist then you should familiarize yourself with the tsunami evacuation protocols.

In case of an earthquake, you should turn into your radio and wait for any tsunami warnings. When a tsunami warning is issued, you need to evacuate immediately, if you have any pets, take them along. Move to higher ground ASAP. You should head inland, away from the coastline. Stay away from the beach in any case. Think about saving yourself and not your valuable possessions. Nothing is precious as human life. You can assist your neighbors who might require special assistance, especially elderly people and infants. Once the tsunami has receded, you can head home only after the local authorities have issued an order saying that it is safe. You should understand that a tsunami is a series of enormous waves. Do not assume that you are out of danger just because one wave has passed; the second wave might be more dangerous than the first one. You can always head to a public shelter in case you feel unsafe at home or when the evacuation warning has been issued.

Avoid areas that were hit and you would want to stay away from such areas because your presence might hinder the rescue operations that might be in way and would put you directly in harm's way. Stay away from all the debris. Check if you got injured and get the necessary first aid before you start helping others. If you think someone needs to be rescued then call for professional help, don't try brave rescues. You can provide any special assistance that others might need. Also stay tuned in to your radio for further announcements. If you notice that any particular building is surrounded by water, then steer clear of the. Be careful when you are re-entering your home or any other buildings. The Tsunami water can cause cracks and damage the foundation of the buildings. Always wear protective clothing and be very careful when you are cleaning up.

Winter storms and extreme cold

The danger that the winter weather might pose differs from region to region. But those who reside in areas that are prone to extreme winter weather need to be prepared for the worst. Winter storms could occur in the form of mild snow or even a heavy blizzard. Most of the winter storms are often accompanied with extremely low temperatures and sometimes strong winds and freezing rains as well. The primary concern during these conditions would be the ability to generate heat, keep the phone lines open and the power flow going. At times due to such severe weather, power supply is generally cut for a few days and even the phone towers are down. It is important that you are prepared for this weather, because most of the deaths that are caused due to this weather are because of traffic accidents on the dangerously icy roads and also of hypothermia. Before winter sets in you should get an emergency kit prepared and remember to include rock salt, shovels, gloves, sand, snow removal equipment and heating fuel. Not just this but you will also need warm clothes and blankets to keep yourself warm.

You will have to make a communication plan with your family regarding the methods that you can make use of for communicating when the normal modes of communication are down. You will also need a radio and extra batteries to ensure that you can keep getting information about the situations outside and also to receive any alerts from the local emergency authorities. You will need to minimize your travel and if you have to travel then ensure that you have got your emergency supplies kit in your vehicle as well. Bring your pets inside when the weather gets really harsh. You should get your vehicle winter ready. Get your mechanic to check the levels of antifreeze, the battery and the ignition systems, fluidity of the brakes, the exhaust system to ensure that there aren't any leaks or broken pipes, fuel and air filters, heater and also the defroster. You will also need to install tires that can handle the rough weather, repair any problems in your windshield, ensure that the thermostat is working and check the oil levels. The emergency kit in your vehicle should have a snow shovel, extra batteries, water, flashlight, spare batteries, a battery powered radio, a small broom, food supplies, blankets and a first aid kit. Also carry some rock salt, rope, flares and a fluorescent flag. You will also need to winterize your home and get all the necessary insulation in place to ensure that your house can also handle the winter storms. During winter storms or even extreme cold, you should stay indoors, when heading outside wear sufficient layers of protective clothing, tread carefully, don't overexert yourself, keep yourself dry, and keep checking for signs of frostbite.

If you detect signs of hypothermia then try getting the body temperature up and seek medical help. Don't travel unnecessarily and even when you do have to travel ensure that you have informed someone of your plan to travel, the route you are likely to take and also the time of arrival along with the name of the destination. Conserve fuel at home. If you are stuck on the road then either you can wait for rescue if a safe location is not nearby or you don't have the suitable clothing to step outside. Pull of the highway and remain in your vehicle, conserve your fuel and try exercising a bit to keep your body temperature normal but don't overexert yourself. After the storm passes by your home might lose power and heat for a few hours or even a couple of days. In case your supplies run out you should head to the nearest public shelter and wait. You should protect yourself from frostbite and hypothermia, keep wearing loose clothing of several layers and stay indoors as much as possible.

Learn from your previous experiences. You can stock up your house better and prepare yourself for future winter storms. Take note of others experiences as well. Try improvising your emergency plans and supplies.

Pandemic

You will be able to prepare for influenza pandemic after this. You should know about not just the magnitude of what is likely to happen during an outbreak but also the actions that can be taken to reduce the impact of influenza pandemic on yourself as well as your family. The information provided in this checklist will provide you all the information that you would need in case of influenza or flu pandemic. While preparing for a pandemic you will need to stock up on at least two weeks of supply of food and water. During a pandemic it is likely that the local stores might either be shut down or they might not have sufficient supplies. So these emergency supplies will come in while handy and it will also help you while preparing for other disasters as well. You will need to keep checking the supply of your prescription drugs regularly to ensure that you will not run out of them anytime soon. Other nonprescription drugs should also be on hand including painkillers, various stomach remedies and medicines for cough, cold and flu. Stock up on plenty of fluids and vitamins. For personal reference you might want to get copies of your health records from your doctor and also maintain them in an electric form as well. You will need to talk to your family members and your loved ones about how they will have to care for the ones who get sick or if they get sick. You can volunteer with any of the local groups and this will help you to prepare yourself about how you will have to respond in case of an emergency. Also get involved in the efforts of your local community that deals with the preparation for influenza pandemic. During the pandemic you will have to take steps to limit the spreading of germs if you want to prevent infection. You can do this by avoiding any form of close contact with the people who are sick. And when you get sick, you should stay away from others and this will protect them from contacting any illness.

If possible, you should stay home when sick. Stay away from work, school or any errands that you had to run, this would help prevent others from catching what you have got. Always cover your nose and mouth while sneezing or coughing as this limits the spread of the harmful germs. Always wash your hands and this will help protect you from the germs you might have caught from someone else. You should avoid toughing your eyes, nose and mouth, because this happens to be the most common way in which germs tend to spread. When you touch something that is contaminated with the harmful germs, you are assisting in their movement when you touch your mouth, eyes and nose with the same hand. You should start practicing healthy habits. Like getting sufficient sleep, engage yourself in physical activity, manage stress effectively, eat healthy and nutritious food also keep drinking plenty of fluids.

10 Survival Tips

Here are ten survival tips that will help you when a disaster strikes.

Tip 1- You need to start with an assumption that a disaster can happen at any given time. Do not assume that it will not happen. Psychology accounts for about 90% of survival, so if you are mentally or even emotionally unprepared then your chances of survival surely go down.

Tip 2- You shouldn't panic. It is natural to be scared during a scenario of survival; if you prepare yourself for such a scenario beforehand then you will be able to deal with the situation effectively. You shouldn't spread fear instead spread information about facts that would come in handy. You can share information about survival training, provided you have gathered your information from sources of repute.

Tip 3- It is important that you know about your limitations. Unless your family consists of soldiers with Special Forces training, they will all have specific needs that you need to keep in mind. You need to create a plan of survival that is specifically designed for your family. You need to take into account considerations such as lack of exercise, special medications, any mobility issues and a various other variables. If you know your limitations then you can make a plan that will help reduce your risk during an emergency and also play to your strengths.

Tip 4- You need to learn how you to make do with less. For instance if you go camping outdoors for a weekend you will learn more about the basics of survival than you would learn if you are sitting in your comfortable living room and reading a book about survival. Practical experience is always better than just theoretical knowledge.

Tip 5- You should keep your plan simple. Having complex and fancy survival preparedness plans and equipment will not really be of much use in a high-pressure scenario. When an emergency occurs you would need a plan that is easy to understand and follow.

Tip 6- You will need to study the disasters that the area you are living in is prone to. With the information that you have gathered you will be able to prepare for the likely disasters. You need to keep in mind that not every place is prone to the same disasters and accordingly you can tweak your plans.

Tip 7- You need to get all your home based supplies in place, along with it you should also create a survival kit for your family and it should contain all the emergency supplies that you would require in case your family has to evacuate at a minutes' notice.

Tip 8- You need to physically prepare yourself to be able t o act upon the preparedness plan you have prepared. Talking is easy, discussing the plan is also easy; unless and until you practice the plan a few times you will not really get a hang of it. You need to keep practicing this plan and don't be afraid to make any necessary changes to the plan. Keep tweaking your plan according to any troubles that you might have faced during the practice session.

Tip 9- Help your neighbors as well. Once you think that you and your family are prepared, you can help your neighbors as well. You can help your entire neighborhood.

Tip 10- Once you are done with your preparation work, you will need to ensure that the items in your survival kit haven't expired. Replace the expired items with fresh ones.

Keep checking your supplies regularly, if you think you need to stock up some additional quantity of items, then go ahead and do so.

Preparedness training for survival should help you get confident that you would be able to deal with any situation; it should not build unnecessary paranoia and hysteria. You should remember that when an emergency sets in you will need to follow your plan and do not panic.

Jack Campbell

Chapter 8

Tips and Points to Remember

In this chapter we look at some pointers to remember when you do go on a survival streak.

1.   Remember to carry the minimum number for things for maximum use. Carry things like small knives, flashlights, cigarette lighter, tissues, and band-aids and so on.

2.   It is a good idea to store water in tanks or barrels at your backyard, alternately carry a bottle to store water.

3.   Always check your supplies to make sure that none of them have expired.

4.   Practice as often as you can. Join prepper's community or club. You can even go for classes, as all these

will make a difference. Also try practicing various situations.

5.   Carry toilet papers. You can use them to start fires with a cigarette lighter, they can double up as tissues, you can even write on them.

6.   Visit the Red Cross in your area. They usually have guides and handy tips for you.

7.   Do not forget to carry iodine, they are very useful in purifying water, getting rid of germs and can help when you get infected.

8.   Always weigh your bag and see for how long you can carry it.

9.   It is a good idea to carry an extra ten percent of the cash that you have, and keep it for emergency purposes. Don't put it in the bank but you can place it in your survival bag.

10.   Freeze milk. Opt to use skimmed milk instead of full fat milk because the fat settles on the top and gets separated. Frozen milk lasts for a long time and during power cuts it becomes really useful.

11.   Remember the rule of 3s, you can go 3 minutes without air, 3 hours without shelter, you can go 3 days without water and 3 weeks without food.

12.   Carry seeds in your survival kit. Seeds might not seem like a comprehensive meal but you can eat them and you can grow them. So they double up for future food. It is a good idea to carry seeds that grow on most terrains and grow in most weathers.

13.   Go for self defense classes, you never know when you will encounter man made disasters like terrorism. Learn how to fight well and carry ammunition if you can. You can prevent further inconveniences like robbers, thieves, and murderers and so on.

14.   Carry shovels no matter what. These are useful as weapons, they come in handy during cooking, they can be used to chop things, they can be used when you are sowing seeds and more importantly if you are stranded and you need help, you can shovel the ground, put leaves and paper in it and then start a fire. These usually serve as signals for people to come to your rescue.

15.   Carry a compass with you.

16.   Learn how to perform CPR and go for first aid classes. This will help in case any one of your family members are in danger.

17.   Always store your important files and documents on cloud, and if you can't do that then store it in your mails, Gmail provides an option to store all your documents. This will help you in case your computer crashes during times of disasters.

Chapter 9
How to Communicate when the Power is down

You will need to figure out a way that will help you keep the communication lines open even when the power grid is down. When there isn't any power, you might find yourself in a situation where you are cut off from news, your family and friends, and more importantly from information. This happens because the modern means of communication we depend on is connected to the grid. And when the grid is down, so is the power supply. This can prove fatal during times of a crisis. Information is critical during the times of crisis and it can hugely influence your chances of survival. Not having a radio, TV or any other means of communication can leave you clueless about the happenings during the aftermath of any disaster, whether natural or man-made.

It definitely is a scary scenario to imagine yourself being cut off from your loved ones. If you don't have a phone without any network coverage or access to data, the chances of even connecting or regrouping with your loved ones becomes increasingly difficult. All you need is a little preparation to make sure that you will not only have access to vital information but also reach out to your family, even when the power is down.

Carry a cell phone

Carrying a cell phone would be your first line of defense. Having a smart phone would come in handy when there is a power outage. It proves to be of great help during the first few hours after a power outage. If a smart phone has been fully charged, it can last for several hours. It is true that cell phone towers need power to operate, but most of the towers are designed in such a way that they have a backup system for power. In the initial hours of a crisis, usually the cell phone networks are up and running. So, you can make use of your cell phone to stay connected. A phone that provides you access to the Internet and also has the facility to text would be the best option. This provides you with several ways to stay in touch with others. Calling might seem simpler, but during an emergency, the call volume is generally high and due to this heavy network traffic you might not be able to place a call. Whereas a text message or even an email make use of fewer resources and this gives you a better chance of contacting whomever you were trying to reach. You also need to keep in mind that the battery life of your phone isn't unlimited. If you don't have a charging point in your vicinity that is functioning, then your phone can be used for only a few hours before its battery is completely drained. It would be helpful if you have a solar charger; you can buy one of these online for less than $30. As long as the cell phone towers are working and there is sufficient sunlight to charge your solar charger, you will be able to make use of your cell phone to stay in touch with others.

How to use your cell phone when the cell phone towers are down

If the cell phone tower goes down, usually your cell phone would also go down along with it. But this isn't necessarily true. With all the technological advancement, there is a new piece of technology that can help keep your cell phone working even when the tower is down. goTenna is an example of this and it will help you in sending text messages and even provide GPS information. Sending text messages even when the towers are down is possible because this works with your smart phone and the wireless Bluetooth to set up a network of communication with all those devices that have goTenna enabled on them. It means that you will be able to stay in touch with your family by making use of your cell phone, even when the cell phone towers are down. If you have a small solar charger, it will be useful for not just charging your phone, but your goTenna as well. And this means of communication is completely secure; anyone who isn't a part of your network cannot listen in.

A landline would be very helpful

Landline phones, especially the older models don't need any power to work. Don't discard them and they aren't completely obsolete. One of these dinosaurs would come in handy during the time of a disaster and it doesn't even require electricity to function. One crucial step that is important to ensure that you are fully prepared is to compile an old fashioned contact book. All the smart phones have made it convenient to store and organize all your contacts. What would you do if your smart-phone dies? This is the reason why it a contact book would come in handy. What good would a telephone do if you don't have the numbers to contact your friends or your family?

Elbow grease!

In the case of any emergency or even a power outage, information is vital. You need to be aware of the happenings around you. Radio announcements along with broadcasts on TV usually provide all the information you need about any local danger or instructions for evacuation and related instructions. Various means of communication are usually down during a major emergency and it would be wise to buy a crank radio. This will provide you with all the information you need even when the power is out. All that is required is a little of elbow grease and once you get the radio to start working you will be able to tune into any of the local news broadcasts.

The one item that should be on your prepper kit

You should have a cable readily available that will allow your computer to directly connect to the Internet. It does not necessarily mean that the Internet is down just because there is a power outage. You need a cable that will let your laptop connect directly to the Internet jack and let you connect to the Internet. A cable is required, not a wireless router. Accessing the Internet will provide you with all the news updates and any other relevant information that might come in handy for your survival.

We live in the age of technology and we are relying heavily on the power grid, than we ever did before. This same technology also provides us with some unusual ideas regarding communication in times of an emergency. Make use of these means and you should be able to put together a back-up plan for communication when all the usual means fail. This could make all the difference to your survival during the collapse of a power grid.

Some devices that might come in handy

Hurricane Sandy, in the year 2012 October wreaked havoc in the regions of New York and New Jersey.

All the lines of communication were down; the power lines were destroyed along with the cell phone towers. Thousands were plunged back to the dark ages without the supply of power. During an emergency, the device that will help you communicate immediately must be in your pocket right now, your cell phone. But we are aware that when the cell phone towers and power are down, communicating through cell phone is not really a viable option. But there is a certain external hardware that is known as GoTenna and it does not need WiFi or even a cell tower to function. It lets you communicate with other GoTenna users by making use of Bluetooth. And as long as the receiver uses GoTenna as well, distance is not really a problem. This is far cheaper and offers a greater degree of mobility than walkie-talkies and HAM radios. During the times of an emergency, power becomes a precious commodity. Even if your phone has got service and reception, but what good will this do if there isn't any charge left in it? This is when a solar charger comes in handy. But a solar charger can be used only when there is some sun, but what about those times when it's cloudy? A device like the BioLite CampStove is portable and lets you charge any device making use of a USB cord by burning any form of biomass that is burnable. Disasters aren't predictable and the best way to cope with them is by being prepared. It is really important that you will be able to communicate with your loved ones to ensure their safety and also inform them about your situation.

Chapter 10
Disaster Supply Kit

In a nutshell, the disaster supply kit consists of all the basic items that you would need in case of an emergency. It will be helpful if you have prepared a kit in advance. During an emergency you might have to evacuate without any notice and that really is not the ideal time to start preparing a supply kit. This kit is not just for the supplies during an emergency, but also for the period following an emergency. You might have to survive on your own and this means that you need to have sufficient food, water and supplies that will last you a minimum of 72 hours. The rescue and relief workers will get to work as soon as possible but this does not guarantee that they will be able to reach everyone immediately; it might take a few hours or even days. Apart from this, basic facilities such as water, electricity, gas, telephones and even sewage treatment might be cut off for a few days or even weeks and in worst case scenarios even longer. So, you need to be fully prepared to survive any situation.

A basic kit

An emergency kit for times of a disaster must contain the following items, if you think anything is important you can always add on to the list.

Water is a must. One gallon is required per person per day for drinking and sanitation. You need to stock up on at least three days worth of water, depending upon the number of persons, store water. You need to have at least 3 days worth of non-perishable food items. A hand crank radio or a battery powered radio, with some extra batteries. You need to have at least one flashlight and some extra batteries. A first aid kit is a must! A whistle when you have to signal for help. To filter out the contaminants you need a dust mask. Plastic sheets and some duct tape too, they can help secure your shelter. Garbage bags, plastic ties and some moist towelettes for personal sanitation. Wrenches, pliers, can opener and scissors. A copy of local maps and a cell phone along with the necessary chargers, mentioned in the previous chapter.

Additional supplies

You might want to add some other items once you have prepared your basic supplies kit. Some of the items that you can include would be any prescriptions medicines, pair of glasses, infant formula, a pack a diapers, some pet food and extra water for your pet, along with some traveler's checks or cash. You will also need to keep a copy of important family documents on hand such as insurance policies and important documents such as identification papers, bank statements and so on in a waterproof bag or container. Bedding material, like a sleeping bag and at least one blanket per person depending upon the general climate of your surroundings. Fresh pair of clothes; consisting of a long sleeved shirt, pants and sturdy shoes. Bleach or household chlorine, these will act as disinfectants and help purify water and a fire extinguisher. Disposable paper cups, plates, towels and other plastic utensils. Items of feminine hygiene and also a few activity books to keep children engaged.

A first aid kit

During an emergency, a first aid kit would always come in handy. It will always come in handy if you are prepared for any injury. You might be hurt or it might be someone you know, so a first aid kit is a must. You can also take a first aid class to learn how to treat minor injuries; this might make a huge difference in times of an emergency. Simply having the following items will help you stop bleeding, fix minor wounds and stop infection. A pair of sterile gloves made of latex or any other material you aren't allergic to. Sterile dressing that will help control bleeding. You need to have some band-aids and antibiotic ointments. Antibiotic towelettes, cleansing agent, eye wash solution, burn ointment and a thermometer.

Coming to prescribed medicines, carry all such medication that you need to take on a daily basis such as insulin, asthma inhalers or pills for diabetes and various heart ailments. The first aid kit should also contain non-prescription drugs such as an aspirin or any other painkiller, antacids, laxatives, anti-diarrhea medicine, anti allergy medication and some glucose. A pair of scissors, tweezers and any form of lubricant must be included.

Ensure that you are regularly replacing the medicines once they have reached their expiry date. You also need to keep in mind the unique needs of various family members such as infants. You will have to include some formula, diapers, feeding bottles, and sachets of powdered milk, various medications prescribed for a baby. If you or any member of your family makes use of dentures and contact lenses, then you will need to add a spare set of each.

You will need to make a plan

Once you have got the disaster survival kit in place, you will also need to make a plan that will tell you what to do in case of an emergency. In case of an emergency or a disaster it is important that your family should be prepared and informed. It is not necessary that you are always together when these events occur; therefore you should have a plan so that you are able to contact and find one another without much trouble. The first thing that you will need to do is meet up with your family members and discuss the plan of action in case of an emergency. Then you will have to identify the responsibilities that will be given to each member of the household and you can all plan and decide. You will also need to take into consideration what you would do if one of the family members might not be able to perform the duty assigned to them due to various reasons. Once you have divided the responsibilities, you will need to plan the course of action that needs to be taken if you get separated during an emergency. In case this happens, then you will need to decide two places for regrouping. Ideally one place should be right outside the house and the second one should be outside the neighborhood. You will have to select an emergency contact, a person who resides outside your immediate vicinity.

The emergency contact information needs to be stored by everyone either in their phones or their contact books. Once you have figured out the basics for regrouping, you will have to develop a plan in case of a possible evacuation. You will have to decide the place and the route you will take to reach your safe haven. You can opt to check into a hotel/motel, go to a relative or a friends place or even go to the evacuation shelter if the situation so demands. Mock drills will help you in practicing your evacuation plan; this should be done twice a year. Drive through the route decided and also look for alternative routes in case the chosen route is not accessible. If you have pets, then you will have to plan ahead for the pet as well, enquire about pet friendly hotels and animal shelters that would be on your possible evacuation routes.

Stay informed

You will have to know about all the relevant information that will help you stay safe. Learn about the types of disasters or various emergencies the area you reside in is prone to. These events could affect only you and your family or your entire neighborhood like a house fire, a medical emergency or an earthquake, tsunami etc. respectively. You will need to identify the method through which the local authorities would provide information during and after a disaster. It could be through a broadcast over the radio, TV or any other means. You will need to be able to distinguish between weather alerts and warnings. You should also know the plan of action to be adopted in case of a disaster. It is essential that at least one member of your household knows how to practice CPR and can use an AED (automated external defibrillator); this training can come in handy during an emergency.

It will also be helpful if you can share your stories and experiences with your family, friends and neighbors. This will help in educating and also in spreading awareness.

Printed emergency contact cards should be made and each family member should have one of these with them at all times. This should contain contact information of all the members of the household. Carry it in your purse or your wallet. Carry it with you so that at the time of an emergency you don't have to search for it.

The maintenance of your kit

The maintenance of your disaster management kit is as important as the preparation of the kit itself. You will need to ensure that all the canned food is stored in a place that is cool and dry, free of any moisture. All the food items need to be stored in airtight plastic or even metal containers that will protect them from pests. Any canned food that is past its expiry date needs to be discarded and replaced with a fresh item. All the stored water and food supplies need to be changed after six months and also write down the date on all the containers. In this manner you will be able to make use of the goods before they go bad. And every year you should update your kit so that it will be able to meet the basic requirements of all your family members. Keep all your supply kits in one place and place them in containers that are easy to carry, like a duffle bag or even a backpack.

You never know when a disaster might occur, so you will need to prep your home, place of work and even your vehicle to ensure that you are always prepared. Here are some tips that you should keep in mind:

Home: the disaster supply kit you have prepared for home needs to contain the essential supplies that will last you three days. And this kit needs to be kept in a place that is easily accessible so that you can at a minutes' notice and also ensure that all your family members know the location of this kit. Also, you can add some supplies that will keep you functioning for two weeks.

Work: you need to prepare a kit that will shelter you at work for at least a day. You need to have supplies of food, water, medicines and the like in your kit. Also, you can keep a pair of comfortable shoes at work that will come in handy when you have to evacuate. It is important to ensure that your kit is in one container that is easy to carry.

Vehicle: in case you are stranded in your vehicle, you need to keep an emergency kit in your car. The kit should consist of jumper cables, flashlights, extra batteries, a first aid kit, all the necessary medications, water that will be sufficient for one person, radio that can help you to tune into emergency broadcasts, car litter or sand, shovel, set of warm clothes complete with socks, gloves, hat and sturdy shoes, blankets and a sleeping bag. Also you will need to have a cell phone, a charger, flares, reflective triangles and some baby formula and diapers if you have a baby.

You need to be prepared for an emergency; the gas should be full and also carry additional fuel. In case of an emergency, call for help and stay put in your car till the help arrives.

Food: You need to stock up on non-perishable foods that would last at least 3 days, select those foods that your family would eat, keep in mind any special dietary requirements, also avoid those foods that make you thirsty, you can stock up on salt free crackers, whole grain cereals and also canned foods. You need to stock up on foods that don't require refrigeration, cooking or any other kind of special preparation. When you are selecting emergency food supplies, opt for canned foods that are ready to eat, protein bars, granola or any other form of dry cereal, peanut butter, dry fruits, nuts, canned juices, non perishable milk that is pasteurized, any form of low salt content crackers and high energy food products.

Food safety: It is not just about stocking up on food, but you will also need to know what you are supposed to do before and also after an emergency to reduce not just illness but also prevent the food from going bad. Power outages are unpredictable and they can occur at any given point of time. The food that is stored in refrigerators and even freezers can become unsafe for consumption if there isn't any electricity. When the temperatures are between 40 and 140°F, this facilitates growth of bacteria that renders food unfit for consumption. You should also be prepared for times when you will have to manage food when there is no power. If you want to be prepared for such a situation then you should have a refrigerator thermometer on hand, dry ice and also a few days stock of ready to eat meals that don't have any special storage needs. When the power goes out you should try and keep the refrigerator doors closed, this can help keep the food cold for at least 4 hours if kept unopened and the temperature at which the refrigerators should be set at for the proper storage of food is 40° F or below. Once the power is back again, you will have to check the temperature inside the refrigerator and the freezer as well, if the temperature reading is 40° F or below, then the food is safe to be consumed or it can be refrozen. Food that has been refrigerated can be safe for consumption if the power is restored within four hours and no more. All the perishable foods like meat, poultry eggs or any leftovers need to be discarded after two hours if the temperature has been above 40° F. You should make it a habit of storing some dry ice in your freezer. When the power goes out, you will be able to keep things cold for an extended period of time by making use of dry ice. You can keep a 10 cubic feet freezer below freezing temperature for a period of up to 4 days by making use of 25 pounds of dry ice. You will need to ensure that your food is in contact with dry ice if you want it to stay frozen and you should wear dry heavy gloves while handling dry ice.

Water: one thing that is absolutely essential for survival is water. Supply of clean drinking water might either be cut off or contaminated after a disaster and you need to be prepared to deal with the water needs of your family. The first step of preparation is to understand the amount of water that you will need to store. It is ideal that you store at least one gallon of water per person for a day, so that makes it 3 gallons per person for the duration of three days. On an average, a human being requires at least three quarters of a gallon of water per day for consumption and various sanitation purposes. But consumption of water would depend upon the level of activity, age and even the climatic conditions. Usually, children, nursing mothers and even sick people tend to require more water and in case a medical emergency crops up, the water requirement might increase. And also depending upon the weather conditions you will have to determine the average water requirement. Whatever the requirement is you will need to store at least a minimum of three days worth of water.

When it comes to storing water, it would be best if you purchase bottled water since this is considered to be the safest of sources. Let the water be in its original container and do not open it until the need presents itself. Also check the expiration date and store it in a cool, dark and dry place. You will have to keep replacing the expired bottles of water with fresh ones. If you want to prepare your own containers of water instead of purchasing bottled water, then you will need to buy food grade storage containers to store water. Before you fill the bottles up with water, you will have to wash the containers and rinse it thoroughly so that there is no residue. If you want to make use of storage containers that you have got at home then make use of the two liter soft drink bottles. Don't make use of the cardboard containers, plastic jugs or any other containers that were used for storing milk or fruit juices. The milk protein and fruit sugar residues are difficult to get rid of. Even glass containers aren't fit for water storage. If you want to store water in the empty plastic soda bottles; you will have to clean them thoroughly with dishwashing soap and sanitize them with any sanitizing agents like household bleach. Once you have got the bottles all cleaned up, fill them up with regular tap water.

If the tap water is from a source that is not treated with chlorine then you will have to add about two drops of non-scented household chlorine based bleach, if the water is treated with chlorine then you can just fill the bottles up. There should be a noticeable chlorine odor, if it isn't there then add another drop or two of the bleach. Tightly seal the bottle with its cap and mark the container so that you know when you filled the bottle up. You can also make use of water purification tablets that are now available. Store the packaged water in a cool dark place. Water that has been bottled needs to be replaced after every six months.

Chapter 11
Disaster Preparedness Tips

Here are ten disaster preparedness tips that will come in handy:

Tip 1: You should know what you would have to face

The first step of being prepared is to have knowledge of likely disasters that you might have to face and also the steps that you will need to take in each such situation. Depending upon the geographical location, you will have to prepare for certain disasters. For instance, if you are living in California, you will need to be prepared for earthquakes but don't ignore other emergencies like severe weather or even a flu pandemic. If you cannot think of all the disasters, then you can always refer to internet. If you think, you are living in an area free from disasters then you need to think again.

Tip 2: Learn about the local evacuation routes and shelters

You need to figure these out well in advance; it really is not the right time to think about these after the tsunami or the hurricane warning has been issued. Evacuations are common and it will come handy if you know the required details well in advance. You should also be acquainted with evacuation routes even the more obscure ones. If you have children, then you can draw a map and post it on their door. This will help them get acquainted with the routes as well. Not just the route for evacuation, you will also have to pan for the meeting point where your family can regroup in case you have to evacuate your house. The location could be right outside your house or even the neighborhood. You will have to decide well in advance about the place you would go to in case of an evacuation; it could be a friend's place, a relative's home or even an evacuation shelter.

Tip 3: How to reconnect with people who matter

If the cell network were disturbed, not being able to stream Netflix wouldn't be your only worry. You will need to think of a way in which you will be able to contact your family and friends. How will you be able to let others know that you are fine? If you figure out a way of doing this well beforehand, dealing with the situation is going to become that much easier. It might be easier to make long distance calls during an emergency, so it would help to have a person listed as emergency contact who doesn't stay in the immediate locality. A list of emergency contacts along with local emergency contacts must be carried by everyone.

Tip 4: Signing up for emergency alerts would be helpful

You will be able to receive emergency alerts on your cell phone, provided you haven't disabled such alerts. The blaring noise of the alerts might be annoying when your phone is on silent mode, but this is the best way to stay informed and even learn about emergencies. Not just this, but the emergency system will also broadcast emergency warnings over the radio and TV. Even a weather radio station will be able to help you stay informed about any severe weather conditions. In this tech savvy age, social media is also considered to be one of the fastest ways to obtain information. But then again, during an emergency you might not even be able to access the internet. So, you will have to think about alternative methods of obtaining information.

Tip 5: Prepare for situations where you are stranded away from home

It is not necessary that you are at home when the emergency strikes. You should be sufficiently prepared to react in a different location when the emergency strikes; you might be in your car or even at work. This consists of very basic stuff like the evacuation routes, a plan for communication and also the manner of receiving the emergency alerts. In case you have children, then you will need to have a plan for regrouping with your children, you should talk to their daycares or schools and gather information about how they would communicate with the family of the child in case of an emergency. Also enquire about any emergency shelter or evacuation routes they would make use of in case of an evacuation.

Tip 6: A disaster supply kit is a must

You need to have some of the basic necessities all in place. This includes food, first aid, water and other emergency equipment that would come in handy. The previous topic dealt with the making and maintenance of a basic supply kid. Read it thoroughly. The kit needs to be assembled and kept in a place that has been decided beforehand, the supplies shouldn't be scattered all over the house. Ensure that the items in the kit are in working condition, the expired items replaced with fresh ones and also that no one has been sneaking snacks out of the kit. Remember one thing, if you don't know how to use what you have got in the kit then the kit becomes useless.

Tip 7: Pay attention to people who might need special preparation

Infants, children, people with disabilities and also seniors should all be taken into consideration when planning for an emergency. If you or any of your family members requires any special attention, medical equipment or even medication, you will have to make sure that you have included such supplies in your kit. And also you might want to talk to your neighbors and discuss how you can help one another during the times of an emergency.

Tip 8: Don't forget about your pets

The goal of prepping for an emergency is to keep your family safe and this includes your pets, if you have got any. In case of an evacuation you will have to make necessary arrangements to take your pet along, you cannot leave them behind. You might want to try and evacuate to a friend's or a relative's house as pets might not be allowed in public evacuation shelters. You will also need to prepare a pet evacuation kit that consists of food and anything else that your pet might require. Micro-chipping your pets might be a good option because it will let you track the moment of your pet through a GPS tracker. Keep a list of shelters that will allow animals.

Tip 9: Learning emergency skills might be a good idea

Little things like how to use a fire extinguisher, giving CPR or performing basic first aid might make a huge difference during the times of an emergency. Getting trained in CPR or even the hands only CPR might come in handy when you least expect it. There are various emergency skills that you can learn by enrolling yourself in workshops or even on the internet.

Tip 10: Helping your community

You should enquire about the ways in which you can help your community during the times of an emergency or a disaster. Most of the time volunteer firefighters are provided training for responding to different emergencies. You can enroll in workshops that will teach you the ways in which you might be able to help your neighborhood. Most of the local emergency agencies as well as non-profit organizations have volunteer positions and you can register as a volunteer.

These ten simple steps will help you be prepared for any disaster.

Jack Campbell

Chapter 12
Financial crisis

Meaning of financial crisis

This can be thought of as a situation where the value of assets or even financial institutions drops quickly. A financial crisis is generally related with panic or a run on the banks, the investors are in a hurry to unload their assets or withdraw their savings with an expectation that the value of those assets is going to decrease if they stay in the custody of a financial institution. A financial crisis could be a result of various things, such as the overvaluation of assets or even institutions, and this could be worsened by the behavior of the investors. When this is coupled with increasing sale of assets at a reduced price as well as withdrawals of savings accounts, it just worsens the situation. When this pattern is left unchecked for a while, it might result in an economic meltdown in the form of recession or even depression.

The three things that you will learn in this chapter are: the actions that you will have to take to get back on back on track financially, process of setting and achieving goals and to understand why it really isn't important to strive for perfection when you are trying to improve your situation. If you think you are the only one who is suffering a financial setback, big or small, you will need to think again. You aren't alone and there indeed is a way out of the mess you are in. given the rocky situation of the economies at present; many people are finding themselves in similar position. Economic meltdown might not be the only reason why you would find yourself in this situation, some popular reasons seem to be overspending, medical bills, bankruptcy and in some cases even divorce seems to be the cause. More people than ever seem to be facing financial crisis these days. It does not really matter what was the cause for the financial setback because the path to recovery is the same for all. Here are the six steps that will help you recover from a financial crisis:

Step 1: Come to terms with your situation

The first step is to accepting the situation you are in and to stop wallowing in grief. Yes, it is sad. Yes, you might be the victim of someone else's mistakes. And yes, it is upsetting. The one thing you need to realize that, all that doesn't really matter anymore. You need to understand that what is done is done and you can't erase it. Instead of resisting the cold reality, accept it. It really helps. When you stop living in the past, only then will you be able to move forward. You need to do this because it is the best possible way that will help you and not because it is the right thing to do. If you keep devoting most of your energy towards wallowing in self-pity, you won't have any left to solve the challenges that you are facing. It indeed is true; the best defense is a good offense. So, stop feeling bad for yourself and focus your energy towards solving the problems.

Step 2: Take stock of your finances

The second step is to take an inventory of your finances. This will help you judge your current situation. If you want to develop a plan of action to get yourself out of the trouble you are in, you will need to know the resources that you have on hand and all the liabilities that are looming over your head. You need to know your current position if you want to get out of it. This is similar to plotting your path on a map. The first thing you should do is find your current location so that you can take the appropriate route to reach your destination. Similarly, on a financial note you need to redefine your starting point and be true to yourself. Some questions that will help you with this step would be; how much do I owe? What are my remaining assets? How much will I need to earn to repay my debts? How much do I spend? How much do I save? And so on. You need to know where you are at present to get to your final destination.

Step 3: You will need to define your goal

The third step is for you to define your objective or the goal of your plan for recovery. Taking the road map analogy a step further, this step is about locating the end destination on the road map. Once you know your location and your destination the only thing left to do is to get started with plotting the most suitable course to reach your goal. The **S.M.A.R.T.** system will provide the necessary guidelines for setting up your destination. S stands for **Specific**; this means that your goals need to be specific and measurable. They shouldn't be vague like I want to earn more money.

This is vague; instead you can define your goal, as "I want to be able to save $1000 per month from January 2016". M stands for **Measurable**; your goals should be capable of being measured, like in the above example the money to be saved per month was denoted in dollars. You can have smaller goals on the road to your final destination. Your goals need to be **Attainable**. The line between setting a goal that will help you push yourself is very fine from setting goals that are simply unattainable. Your goals should let you stretch yourself and should also be capable of being achieved. If not, then all you are doing is setting up yourself for failure. Your goals need to be **Realistic**. For instance you are neck deep in credit card debt and you are filing for bankruptcy, it is not realistic to set a goal that you will become a millionaire within one year. Is it? And lastly, your goal needs to have a **Time limit**. A goal that has no deadline seems like wishful thinking. It won't be considered as a smart goal if there is no time limit set. People tend to work better when they have a deadline to adhere to.

Step 4: Start developing your plan

After you have managed to set your goal, the next step is to start working on developing a plan to achieve your goal. You need to figure out a plan that will help you bridge the gap between your present position and your future destination. You need to figure out the most efficient route to get there. One thing you need to do is to ensure that you the process you have adopted is fulfilling. Often people think of it as an obligation, yes it is an obligation, but you need to take into consideration your sense of satisfaction as well. One suitable solution for this problem is that you can repay your debt and along with it add in some retirement savings or even some assets. When you do this you are providing yourself an emotional boost, while staying on track to financial recovery.

Step 5: Start taking action

The fifth step is for you to start taking action. This sounds obvious, doesn't it? But in reality, for some unknown reason people tend to forget this step. Your plan for financial recovery will remain as a figment of wishful thinking unless it has been put into action. Nothing is going to happen, if you don't take any action. Only a few tend to take steps that will help them reaching their goals, this is what makes all the difference.

Step 6: Make corrections and adjustments

Once you have put your plan into action, only then will you be able to learn from

both your experiences and mistakes. You will not only improve your skills but your knowledge as well. You can keep making amendments and improvements to your plan as and when you think it's necessary. You needn't concentrate on achieving perfection, your plans might be flawed, but you will realize all this only when you put it into action. And you will definitely learn from your mistakes. So, it is perfectly all right that you think your plan needs to be tweaked. Make the necessary changes and stay on track towards financial recovery. But you will need to start immediately. If you don't start now, then there's no scope for making any changes. These six steps will definitely help you out of you financial slump.

Jack Campbell

Conclusion

Thank you for choosing and buying this book. I hope you enjoyed this book and hope that this book gave you a good insight on what surviving is all about. Disasters always cause several inconveniences and you often will find yourself cut off from the basic facilities and necessities. Rehabilitation is something that is hard and surviving is harder. It is important to therefore be well prepared to face any challenging situation head on. It is mentally exhausting and physically enduring, but with little preparation and points to remember you will be able to make it through. It isn't just loss of life and property, but it can result in loss of electricity, lack of supply of provisions, lack of medicine and no infrastructure facilities.

With this book I am sure you got an overview on how disasters affect people and why prepping is a necessity and a key in surviving even the most difficult of times. You would have also got adequate knowledge on how to hunt, fish, can and forage. In the end of the day, remember to maintain a calm mind, a hopeful heart and practical knowledge to get out of situations. Remember that you are responsible for your survival and your recovery. Thank you once again for purchasing this book.

Thank you for Reading! I Need Your Help...

Dear Reader,

I Hope you Enjoyed "**Survival: Prepper's Survival Guide - Hunting, Fishing, Canning, and Foraging**". I have to tell you, as an Author, I love feedback! I am always seeking ways to improve my current books and make the next ones better. It's readers like you who have the biggest impact on a book's success and development! So, tell me what you liked, what you loved, and even what you hated. I would love to hear from you, and I would like to ask you a favor, if you are so inclined, would you please share a minute to review my book. Loved it, Hated it - I'd just enjoy your feedback.

As you May have gleaned from my books, reviews can be tough to come by these days and You the reader have the power make or break the success of a book. If you'd be so kind to review the book, I would greatly appreciate it!

Thank you so much again for reading "**Survival: Prepper's Survival Guide - Hunting, Fishing, Canning, and Foraging**" and for spending time with me! I will see you in the next one!

Free Bonus!!!

We would like to Offer you Exclusive access to our Breakthrough Book Club!!! It's a place where we offer a NEW FREE E-book every week! Also our members are actively discussing, reviewing, and sharing their thoughts on the Book of The Week and on topics to help each other Breakthrough Life's Obstacles! With a Chance to win a $25 Gift Card EVERY Month! Please Enjoy Your FREE Access: https://www.facebook.com/groups/BreakthroughBookClub/

Check Out More From The Publisher…

Healthy Living: Mental Health, Find Happiness by Improving your Gut Health, Sugar Addiction, and IBS

by Maria Lexington

http://www.amazon.com/Healthy-Living-Happiness-Schizophrenia-Fibromyalgia-ebook/dp/B010KM9CLA

Investing: Stocks, Options, Gold & Silver, Your Path To Wealth In A Bull Or Bear Stock Market

by Warrick Liversedge

http://www.amazon.com/Investing-Options-Financial-Passive-Dividends-ebook/dp/B015T8GCSG

Social Media: Master Social Media Marketing - Facebook, Twitter, YouTube & Instagram

by Grant Kennedy

http://www.amazon.com/Social-Media-Marketing-Facebook-Instagram-ebook/dp/B018Y68SWS

Gardening: Hydroponics for Beginners: The Ultimate Guide to Hydroponic Gardening

by Melissa Honeydew

http://www.amazon.com/Hydroponics-Sufficiency-Vegetables-Homesteading-Preservation-ebook/dp/B01508IZAS

Psychology: Hypnosis & Mind Control – To Overcome Stress, Anxiety, Depression & Finally Recover Your Happiness

by Fred McGaughy

http://www.amazon.com/Psychology-Hypnosis-Depression-Happiness-Brainwashing-ebook/dp/B014AMVA3E

Jack Campbell

www.ingramcontent.com/pod-product-compliance
Lightning Source LLC
Chambersburg PA
CBHW072206280526
45788CB00002B/895